T0067888

ANSWERIN' THE CALL: MOTHER NATURE'S FIRST RESPONDER

A RUTGER GRADUATE AN AUGUSTA FAVORITE

Antonio Burdette

Order this book online at www.trafford.com
or email orders@trafford.com

Most Trafford titles are also available at major online book retailers.

© Copyright 2022 Antonio Burdette.
All rights reserved. No part of this publication may be reproduced, stored in a retrieval
system, or transmitted, in any form or by any means, electronic, mechanical, photocopying,
recording, or otherwise, without the written prior permission of the author.

Print information available on the last page.

ISBN: 978-1-6987-1247-5 (sc)
ISBN: 978-1-6987-1246-8 (e)

Because of the dynamic nature of the Internet, any web addresses or links contained in
this book may have changed since publication and may no longer be valid. The views
expressed in this work are solely those of the author and do not necessarily reflect the
views of the publisher, and the publisher hereby disclaims any responsibility for them.

Any people depicted in stock imagery provided by Getty Images are models, and such images
are being used for illustrative purposes only.
Certain stock imagery © Getty Images.

Check-in-Coordinator: Eve Ardell
Publishing Services Associate: Josh Laluna
Cover Design: Jay Tinam-isan

Trafford rev. 10/19/2022

www.trafford.com
North America & international
toll-free: 844-688-6899 (USA & Canada)
fax: 812 355 4082

THE PERSON I'M ABOUT to introduce further to the public has to be acknowledged for so many outstanding accomplishments. How can one person set so many goals and not appear frustrated at any point. It's important that **Ms. Jane**

Minar, not be hidden in the background when there are thousands of children who has the exact same interest of desiring to become a devoted meteorologist in Science.

We have to get the point across to **developing minds** that nothing is as hard as it seems when you have someone who clearly understands. Her work ethic speaks for itself each morning as she keeps us updated and passionately prepare us to seek safety when great storms are rapidly transpiring amongst neighboring States.

Ms. Minar is truly a blessing when it comes to the stations she has worked, being able to read a Doppler Rader and Weather board as difficult as that sound. I'm addressing **Ms. Minar** because its easy for people like her to continue to become successful and fade more into their own life. It's not a question, she clearly loves people. These are the type of people that you put high upon a pedestal as if she's a valuable collection vase that you never want to see **broken.**

What a young adult can learn from her they'll take it with them throughout their life because she teaches through values. When you love your job, it shows and a number of her acquaintances can voust that fact.

She learnt from her teacher how to be a teacher and not just remain as a student. It's obvious that **Ms. Jane Minar** grew up before her time and I'm not saying it in a derogatory way, I'm saying it in a way for someone to have that much passion just in learning what seems difficult alone.

She's an advocate for women Stem; Science, Technology, Engineering, and Mathematics. She's an advocate for women who experience domestic violence and her heart is never far from the Children's as she mention what the temperature will be at the bus stop addressing the fact using the phrase "Our Children" a lot of people get into certain fields and 2-3 years – in they announce that they seeking work elsewhere doing something different but hearing her speak while navigating the screen she's a natural and it seems like she study without acknowledging it.

Good honest people are hard to find and when you come across them, you have to figure out what's a special way to keep influencing them with similar like energy.

Although, **Ms. Minar** is a meteorologist, she hears firsthand about news that'll make you cringe somehow she has always managed to remain professional. I have yet to hear her being opinionated it's almost as if her co-workers know not to offset her talent. Which makes them genuine. Clearly, there's more about her that she could use to straight out captivate you but she rather come off to you as being **"basic"** because she's very attractive and easy on the eyes one should be careful being confident isn't a energy that she feels the need to pacify.

Even though she shares the same liking of meteorology with other in her field she's an achiever when it comes to setting the bar high. She leaves no stone unturn when it comes to **the safety of her viewers.** It's almost as if she has a block on when it comes to the risk people take such as riding through flood waters or beach goers out surfing in extremely high tides, her negative comment is to further encourage safety perhaps that's a gift from Augusta, Ga. Living in the home of the masters.

And even though what she does seem to come natural future meteorologist, you have to know that she's putting in the overtime crammin' or for lack of better words "she geekin' out". She's not just a in-the-studio correspondence, she's known for aiding food drives, supporting her love for the game of baseball, our homeroom hitters, the Augusta Green Jackets and her favorite the Phillies she promoted local eateries with nothing more than her honest opinion she even interviewed the brave hearted "Blue Angels" and the reason for this book of encouragement because its not likely for her to brag she rather show you that hardwork pays off and the benefits are limitless. On the air she often mention.

Some of the things that she likes but its so much more about her that we don't know she has a love for cumulus clouds, gorgeous sunrises, wind patterns and you can most certainly second guess yourself. This can possibly make a outside date seem like just another work assignment when you watch how well she delivers the forecast you must first think of the positive influences that knew first hand what it was like to keep her focused and balanced.

Jane Minar is definitely a carbon copy of whomever she decided to pursue meteorology from and not to take from her, she has branched out on her own like something that grows abundantly and rapid.

You must realize **Ms. Minar** stepped in claiming nothing but professionalism, we have to allow those that's great within generations to help fashion our lives because what is learnt is always kept and what is ignored will always be regretted. I can't say enough good things about **Jane Minar** and that's because she's dedicated and devoted when it comes to **the safety of others.** There are many more who don't consider what they do as work, they just step in from the future and they see what it is that needs to be done and they do because the reward is so much greater than the retirement.

Because a large percentage of people she had forewarned have become distraught and agitated from having to start from scratch and rebuild its only fair that we say thank you, recognizing **Ms. Minar** for the energy that keeps her pursuing the phenomenal world without breaking down when she clearly knows that lives has been loss and hearing about the next day death toll of the less fortunate.

What more can you ask for from a woman who lives a freedom filled life, all stemming from her childhood love how *mother nature's way of gathering us and keepin' us on our toes and she clearly understands that it's nothing personal. When the seasons change and different elements at some point has to interact.*

Some reaction gives us beautiful sunrises, amazing sunsets, rainbows, water spouts, and run for cover tornadoes and hurricanes.

This is just a hypothesis (an educated guess) I'm starting to think that she's the reason it gets so damn hot downsouth.

Because **Ms. Minar** has lossed some viewers and has led millions to safety, its only right to recognize how humanitarian someone can be. She has shown time after time that she doesn't stay put where its always pleasant, she gets a thrill out of livin' in the unthinkable **sharin'** the people's unmanageable situations.

She's a brave heart, she'll sail on not so still waters or fly upside down with stunt pilots, she runs yearly marathon(s) in honor of those we've lossed and it seems like she'll support whichever charity that's holding a outside event. I have to give a big shout out to so many women who has found their calling in life at one point women was relying on the men to be the provider but now they have made the message clear that they're just as impactful as anyone else.

There's nothing personal between **Ms. Minar** and I just a platonic relationship of how much she has achieved in the field of meteorology and science. As I said earlier, these great examples don't always remain on the screen for us to continue learning from. They go on to live their lives and we miss out on the simple methods they brought to the screen that helped them achieve greatness. Greatness is still probably an understatement knowing she hasn't reveal all that she knows but greatness speaks volumes when it comes to finding out what it was that she desired to do and making it happen.

This type of person is what young adults need when it comes to pursuing career goals and making someone else's lives a bit easier. Hardwork pays off and she's proving that each time she forewarns us of the natural phenomenonals that this world has to offer. I guess this is my way of askin the Lord to allow me to search for the right type of friends even as I pursue my goals as a inspiring motivational speaker. You can never learn too much but you can always get comfortable and do less. You don't necessarily have to pray over someone to jump start them all over again, I hope that this guide will always remind you of how grateful we are to have a dedicated meteorologist to help us get our family and our family friends to safety when the unexpected decides to show up. We always say my time whining down but in actuality, we'll do it all over again, no questions asked. Each day that I work, I see how enthusiastic these young chefs are and I address them as that instead of allowing them to think that they're just another line cook when there's no gap between you and the profession you claimin'. There's no room for failure. I stay encouraging them because I've worked and lived longer to know how all this work you could be good at what you do and all the while just whined up used and burnt out.

I think **Ms. Minar** knows that a child isn't just the future she knows that their safety will require being precise and accurate when it comes to assisting Fema, Red Cross, and other Emergency Responders to help keep them alive and well. It's not just that she's in a studio broadcasting she chose a field where she can be all over without being judgmental or without prejudice concerning quick thinking survival urgency. I'm most definitely choosing my words carefully honoring a woman of her statue and hopefully the rest of the world will catch on that unconditional love saves lives in abundance. I've said this once before that you cant always choose someone based on a sexual interest the one choice when choosing someone you have to value their qualities that so many miss out on.

Because I lost my baby brother, perhaps I wanna selectively choose a friend. A lot of the time, we do things without reason, but you don't need a reason to show someone how much you appreciate them. Just because **Ms. Minar** is a meteorologist, it seems she understand why Christ chose 12 disciples whose main objective is to **"save"** and that's just another quality that she has that the majority of us overlook sometimes what's hidden has no choice but to surface causing everyone else to look in amazement as if she's doing something out of the ordinary.

We all have been dealt a hand, it's up to you how you play it. You can sit across from your opponents and get bluffed and take the gamble or you can play your hand accordingly and win your books fair and square.

You can't make an assessment about someone unless you studied how they move, their behavior and their motives and we all should now know that her motives is to learn the patterns of Mother Nature and lead her viewers to a promised next day.

Why are people almost forced to say *"I love you enough too"*, when each day they show you through their actions.

I'm no better than anyone else but my eyes are open to those that run a tight ship who wakes up knowing what's needed when it comes to assisting another. You can work anywhere for anybody and gain a paycheck but what good is it if satisfying a human isn't the main objective.

We all know the story of the ant and the grasshopper one played around while the other went tunnel vision workin'. **Jane Minar** is not a "I tried to warn you" type of person, she's a "This storm is rapidly developing, have your emergency kits close by and go to a safe place, this storm is hours away" type of person. And if we weren't so indecisive, you can see that meteorologists can warn you 'til they blue in the face, its up to you to get your family to safety. I've never have yet to hear **Ms. Minar** speak on the viewers she has lost but I can almost promise you it'll be a testimony filled with passion knowing she wants those states that constantly get hit to know that she's apologetic for their loss.

My grandma used to tell me if you see someone in need it's alright to help them cause you never know who it could be. Losses hurt more than physical damage and physical damage leaves scars called **"reminders"**, every storm survivor has some kind of reminder whether if it's physically or mentally. Some viewers take warning lightly a warning is a subliminal message demanding your attention and in this case, it's an angel on the other end of the horn.

You can tell that I'm enthused to know of **Jane Minar**, just though television networking. It's hard to evacuate everyone when a phenomenon appear, hopefully, this book will help her get the help she needs from sponsors to give transportation aid to our elderly, our children, our foreign exchange students and anyone else who share a liking in Humanitary. We must work and we must work harder than we ever had to, to make up for those who wasted valuable time indulging themselves in other practices. You can never let someone kill your spirit because your spirit is the key to manifestin' your dreams.

Because **Ms. Minar** wakes up in the land of the living she dedicate her chosen time/career for those that desire to live beyond their unexpected time line.

Again, help me acknowledge **Ms. Jane Minar,** just on the effort and years she has invested when it comes to still being able to walk amongst so many who has survived mother nature's ordeal.

Proceeding from this self-published book is meant for **Ms. Jane Minar**, in helping her further her career, living arrangements, when it comes to increasing her education in whatever line of work she chooses. Ask yourself how many managers on a job knows first hand how hard you work but will never mention you for a pay increase. I take it upon myself to notice her ambition and not allow her to be at a stand still waiting for someone to finally notice.

When you surround yourself, around the right people bonds get made and forces become unbreakable and because we stay focus on what really matters others has to put in the same amount of effort. Because we lose, generations all the time it's wise to follow someone who has it all together because you don't wanna miss out on important factors that will help you later on in life. Not one time did we mentioned meteorologist as being essential workers. They are amongst the top three working around the clock studying and mapping the paths of Mother Nature, incredible forces leaving you with results of an early warning to seek safety. If meteorologist wasn't fascinated with climate behavior you **couldn't** imagine what the death toll would be based off of a natural disaster. Whether if it's excessively hot or blistering cold, they always have our best of interest and clearly you must acknowledge **Jane Minar** for choosing her career with purpose. The accusations that I'm addressing about **Ms. Jane Minar** are my very own and I hope that this book gives her the strength each morning to keep us safe as possible.

Ms. Minar saving lives is a big deal and although you may not see it as that your hardwork, dedication and courageous behavior deserves more than a thank you and here's my way of saying though you maybe tired keep teachin' 'til you reach beyond the stars and except all that the father has for you cause you deserve it because you share meteorology with a few others you somehow manage to find away, to stand alone, proclaiming your independence. Always be proud of yourself from what you have accomplished and never look back having regrets.

Just your effort and dedication alone got you noticed. It takes unconditional love to warn us about heat that will cause you to become dehydrated, burn time just from being in the heat, temperatures that activates RIP currents, on extremely hot days seek cooling shelters, solar eclipses, droughts, the migration of sharks on local beaches, wildfire and the inches rain will fall without you even acknowledging it, what's the best sunscreen for you and your child, lightning strikes, down power lines, and she serves as a friendly reminder when it comes to triple digit heat and vehicles* and a whole lot more without you, this whole weather agenda wouldn't be nothing but another "guessing game". From a young girl fascinated with the world's elements to a professional meteorologist, you make life easier and interesting just by "Answering the Call: As Mother Nature's very own First Responder".

Printed in the United States
by Baker & Taylor Publisher Services